THE INCREDIBLE SECRET FORMULA BOOK

Make Your Own Rock Candy, Jelly Snakes, Face Paint, Slimy Putty, and 55 More Awesome Things!

SHAR LEVINE & LESLIE JOHNSTONE

Troll

Thanks to our kid testers! (and Kathleen Imanishi!)

Sidney Fischman
Danny Friedman
Richard and Christian Hasbrouck
Zarina Kahn
Max, Zoe, and Kate Mays
River Scott

Published by Troll Communications L.L.C.

The Incredible Secret Formula Book is produced by becker&mayer!, Kirkland, Washington.
www.beckermayer.com

Edited by Marcie DiPietro.
Designed by Matt Hutnak.
Production management by Barbara Galvani.

Printed in the United States of America.

ISBN: 0-8167-7011-5

10 9 8 7 6 5 4 3 2 1

TABLE OF CONTENTS

•INTRODUCTION•

Welcome to the cool world of gooey, slimy, yucky, and really strange concoctions. While this book has been designed with kids in mind, adults will have as much fun with the activities as children. Most of the materials you'll need are probably in your kitchen or bathroom. A quick trip to the grocery store or drugstore will provide the rest of the items required for these simple projects. You may want to save some clean plastic jars; they make perfect storage containers for the finished products.

Although all the activities are safe, children should always be closely supervised while preparing the concoctions in this book. Before beginning a project, please read through all the instructions to make sure you understand each step. It's a good idea to have your materials on hand before you start, so you don't have to go searching for a missing ingredient in the middle of the project.

Despite the names of some of the activities, nothing is really so messy that a wet cloth, a damp mop, or even a hand-held vacuum won't suffice for the cleanup. And remember, any of the projects can be done outdoors in nice weather! Put your apron on, gather your ingredients, and get ready to have fun!

GROCERY LIST

Alum: Spice Aisle or Drugstore
Beeswax: Craft Store
Borax: Laundry Products Aisle
Corn Syrup: Baking Aisle (look near syrups and molasses)
Citric Acid: Grocery Store (usually in aisle with canning supplies)
Epsom Salts: Drugstore (usually in aisle with bath salts, bubble baths)
Glycerine: Drugstore (usually in aisle with cod-liver oil)

TWB (The World's Best) Play Dough

This is it! The original, the one and only amazing dough to play with. We have tried many different recipes, and we think this one is the best!

WHAT YOU WILL NEED

Ingredients

- 1 cup (.24 l) flour
- 1 cup (.24 l) water
- 1 or 2 drops food coloring
- 1/2 cup (.12 l) salt
- 1 tablespoon (14.8 ml) oil
- 2 teaspoons (9.9 ml) cream of tartar

Equipment

- measuring cups & spoons
- saucepan
- wooden spoon
- floured board
- resealable plastic bag

1. Mix together all the ingredients in a saucepan. Have an adult heat the ingredients at medium until the mixture just starts to cook, stirring while it heats. When it is done, it should form a ball and look like sticky play dough.

2. Dump the play dough out onto a floured board and let it sit until it is cool enough to handle safely. Knead it by pushing it down and away from you and folding it over, until you have a smooth dough.

3. Mold the play dough into interesting shapes and figures. When you are finished, store your play dough in a resealable plastic bag.

Adult Help

Give Me All Your Dough

After making dough, you usually need to clean up with soap and water. This dough lets you skip one step because the soap is already in the dough!

WHAT YOU WILL NEED

Ingredients

- 2 cups (.48 l) flour
- 1/2 cup (.12 l) salt
- 2 teaspoons (9.9 ml) liquid tempera paint
- 1 tablespoon (14.8 ml) liquid soap
- 3/4 cup (.18 l) water

Equipment

- measuring cups & spoons
- bowl
- spoon
- resealable plastic bag

1. Mix together the flour, salt, paint, and liquid soap in a bowl.

2. Add water to the dough until it is stiff but sticky. Knead the dough by pushing it down and away from you and folding it over.

3. Model the dough into different shapes. You can store the dough in a resealable plastic bag. When the dough begins to dry out, throw it away and make a fresh batch.

Adult Help

Don't Eat

•**6**•

Dough Nuts

By this time, you're a dough nut! This dough is shiny, smooth, and silky, and you'll like it!

WHAT YOU WILL NEED

Ingredients

- 1/2 cup (.12 l) cornstarch
- 1 cup (.24 l) baking soda
- 3/4 cup (.18 l) water
- food coloring

Equipment

- measuring cups
- saucepan
- spoon
- floured board
- resealable plastic bag

1. Place the cornstarch and baking soda in a saucepan and mix them together.

2. Add the water and mix well.

3. Have an adult cook the mixture over low heat, stirring occasionally, until it looks like mashed potatoes.

4. Let the mixture cool. Gather it with a spoon and plop it onto a floured board.

5. Knead the dough by pushing it down and away from you and folding it over. You can add a drop or two of food coloring at this point to make it an interesting color, then knead some more.

6. Mold the dough into different shapes. You can store the dough in a resealable plastic bag. When the dough begins to dry out, throw it away and make a fresh batch.

Adult Help

Beadworks Dough

Make some colorful beads to wear or to give as gifts. Really tiny beads are good for bracelets and bigger ones make terrific pendants for necklaces.

WHAT YOU WILL NEED

Ingredients

- 3/4 cup (.18 l) flour
- 1/2 cup (.12 l) salt
- 1/2 cup (.12 l) cornstarch
- 1/2 cup (.12 l) water

Equipment

- measuring cups
- bowl
- spoon
- toothpick
- paints & paintbrush
- string

1. Mix the flour, salt, and cornstarch in a bowl. Slowly add the water, mixing until the dough holds a shape. (Note: You may not need all the water.)

2. Knead the dough in the bowl by pushing it down and away from you and folding it over.

3. Roll small pieces of dough between your hands to make beads.

4. Poke a toothpick through each bead to make a hole. Take out the toothpick and allow the beads to dry. Drying time depends on the size of your beads. Small beads will dry in a few hours; larger ones will need to sit overnight.

5. Paint the beads. When the beads are dry, you can string them to make jewelry.

Adult Help

Long Time   **Don't Eat**

● 8 ●

Amazing Eggshell Chalk

We guarantee that this is the most fun you can have with a dozen eggs. This chalk works equally well on sidewalks and on chalkboards. If you have difficulty using up a dozen eggs, ask an adult if he or she knows how to make angel food cake—another good reason to make this chalk!

WHAT YOU WILL NEED

Ingredients

- eggshells from 12 eggs
- 2 teaspoons (9.9 ml) flour
- powdered tempera paint (optional)
- 2 teaspoons (9.9 ml) hot water

Equipment

- measuring spoons
- resealable plastic bag
- rolling pin or bottle
- small bowl
- spoon

1. Carefully wash the eggshells, removing any attached membranes, and dry them.

2. Put the shells into a resealable plastic bag and use a rolling pin or bottle to crush the shells to a fine powder.

3. Pour the powdered eggshells into a bowl. Add the flour and some paint, and mix together until the color is consistent throughout. Add the water and mix to form a paste. Roll the paste into a tube shape and allow it to dry overnight before using.

Adult Help   Long Time   Don't Eat

Party Piñatas

Breaking piñatas is the only time it's acceptable to whack a piece of art. Fill with goodies and enjoy!

WHAT YOU WILL NEED
•PASTE•

Ingredients

- 1/4 cup (.06 l) sugar
- 1/4 cup (.06 l) flour
- 1/2 teaspoon (2.5 ml) alum
- 2 cups (.48 l) water, divided

Equipment

- measuring cups & spoons
- saucepan
- spoon

•PASTE•

1. Mix the sugar, flour, alum, and 1 cup (.24 l) water in a saucepan.

2. Have an adult bring this mixture to a boil, stirring while it heats. Cook until it is clear.

3. Let the mixture cool, then add the additional 1 cup (.24 l) water and mix well.

•PULP•

1. Rip, shred, and generally mince the napkins and tissues into tiny bits. Put them in a large plastic bucket or container.

2. Dump the paste in and mix well. Now you're ready to start creating!

WHAT YOU WILL NEED
•PULP•

Ingredients

- different kinds of light-weight paper (napkins, toilet paper, crepe, tissue, etc.)
- homemade paste (recipe on this page)

Equipment

- large plastic bucket or container

Adult Help

Long Time   **Don't Eat**

WHAT YOU WILL NEED
•PIÑATA•

Equipment

- balloon
- old wastepaper basket
- newspaper
- wrapped candies
- paints & paintbrush
- string or rope

•PIÑATA•

1. Blow up a balloon. Rest the balloon on the rim of an old wastepaper basket to hold it steady as you work.

2. Tear the newspaper into long strips. Pull the strips through the pulp/paste mixture until the strips are completely coated.

3. Cover the balloon with the coated strips. Leave a space around the mouth of the balloon just large enough to put candies through.

4. Add more layers of newspaper strips until you have completed five or six layers and can no longer see the balloon. Allow this to dry completely. (This will take 3 to 4 days.)

5. When the newspaper is dry, pop the balloon and remove it from the piñata. (Carefully throw away <u>all</u> the pieces.) Drop in the candies, then close off the hole with more gooey strips or masking tape.

6. Paint the piñata and hang it in a wide-open space. You know what to do now!

IDEAS FOR CREATING A UNIQUE PIÑATA:

Piñatas can be made to look like anything. Easy designs include soccer balls or baseballs, which are just round balloon shapes with painted-on designs. Pufferfish are also fun and easy: Make a round fish body, paint, and glue on layers of crepe paper to look like scales and fins. For other shapes, make a frame on the balloon using pieces of egg carton and masking tape, then layer the newspaper strips over the top. For example, to make a pig, use the egg carton pieces for feet and a snout. When the newspaper strips are dry, paint the pig and add construction paper eyelashes and a curly tail. Any type of paint that works on paper can be used; washable tempera paints are always a good choice for easy cleanup!

Do-It-Yourself Face Paint

Have you ever dreamed of being a cat, a princess, or an alien? When you get tired of being yourself, try painting on a new face. It is guaranteed to make you smile. Here is an easy way to make face paint so you can be whatever you want to be!

WHAT YOU WILL NEED

Ingredients

- 1/2 teaspoon (2.5 ml) cold cream or face cream
- 1 teaspoon (4.9 ml) cornstarch
- 1/2 teaspoon (2.5 ml) water
- food coloring

Equipment

- measuring spoons
- small containers with lids
- spoon
- small paintbrush

1. Mix together the cold cream and cornstarch in a small plastic container until they are well blended. Add the water drop by drop, stirring until the mixture is creamy. (Note: You may not need all of the water, depending on the face cream used.)

2. Stir in food coloring one drop at a time until the desired color is achieved. Don't put in too many drops! Really strong colors can stain your skin temporarily. Repeat steps 1 and 2 for as many colors as you'd like to make.

3. Paint designs on your face with a small paintbrush.

4. Use soap and water to clean your face afterward. Cover and store any remaining paint.

Adult Help

Don't Eat

Ten-Finger Fun

Nothing is quite as much fun as finger painting. And nothing makes as much of a mess! Use plastic tablecloths for drop cloths and wear old clothes. Instead of using finger-painting paper, which can be expensive, try freezer paper—it comes by the roll and is shiny on one side.

WHAT YOU WILL NEED

Ingredients

- 3 tablespoons (44 ml) sugar
- 1/2 cup (.12 l) cornstarch
- 2 cups (.48 l) cold water
- 1 teaspoon (4.9 ml) liquid dishwashing detergent
- food coloring

Equipment

- measuring cups & spoons
- saucepan
- spoon
- small plastic containers with lids

1. Mix the sugar and cornstarch together in a saucepan. Add the water, and have an adult cook this mixture over low heat, stirring continuously until it is thick.

2. Remove the mixture from the heat and stir in the detergent.

3. Divide the mixture evenly among several small plastic containers. Use different combinations of food coloring to give each container a unique color.

4. Stir well and use when the paints have cooled. Cover and store any remaining paint.

Adult Help

Don't Eat

Got Paint?

You know that milk does a body good, but did you know it makes great pictures, too? This is not something to drink; it's something you can use to paint!

What You Will Need

Ingredients

- 1 tablespoon (14.8 ml) nonfat powdered milk
- 1/2 cup (.12 l) water
- 1 teaspoon (4.9 ml) powdered tempera paint

Equipment

- measuring cups & spoons
- small plastic containers with lids
- spoon

1. Place the powdered milk and water in a plastic container. Mix and let stand until the bubbles have disappeared.

2. Stir in the tempera paint. Repeat steps 1 and 2 for as many colors as you'd like to make.

3. Paint up a storm! When you are finished, you can clean off the sides of the containers, cover, and store in the fridge for up to two weeks. Make sure you label the containers: PAINT.

Adult Help

Don't Eat

Monet Watercolor

Claude Monet was a famous French painter who created amazing pictures of gardens. Maybe he got started with watercolors just like this.

What You Will Need

Ingredients

- 1 tablespoon (14.8 ml) white vinegar
- 2 tablespoons (29.6 ml) baking soda
- 1 tablespoon (14.8 ml) cornstarch
- 1/4 teaspoon (1.2 ml) glycerine
- food coloring

Equipment

- measuring spoons
- bowl
- spoon
- small plastic containers

1. Have an adult mix the vinegar and baking soda together in a bowl. (Looks like a volcano, doesn't it?)

2. When the mixture stops foaming, add the cornstarch and glycerine and stir.

3. Pour the mixture into a small plastic container, stir in a drop or two of food coloring (watch how the color changes!), and let it sit overnight to harden. Repeat steps 1 through 3 for as many colors as you'd like to make.

4. Dip a paintbrush in water, then use the colors to paint your own masterpiece.

•15•

Adult Help   Long Time   Don't Eat

Invisible Ink #1

Here is a ghostly ink that will also leave a scent. There's a civilized method of doing this and a gross one. Let's try the nice one first.

WHAT YOU WILL NEED

Ingredients

- a fresh lemon or onion

Equipment

- knife
- small bowl
- cotton swab
- white paper
- lamp

1. Have an adult cut and squeeze the lemon or puree the onion in a blender and pour the juice into a small bowl.

2. Dip a cotton swab into the liquid and write your secret message on a piece of white paper.

3. Allow the paper to dry. Don't place it anywhere warm!

4. When the "ink" is completely dry, hold the paper near something warm, like a lamp or a heat register. Don't get too close—you don't want the paper to catch fire!

5. Watch as your message magically appears.

the gross version:

Let's say you were held captive in a tower and you had nothing with which to write. You have to get a message to your friends. What can you do? Use sweat or saliva instead of lemon or onion juice. Yuck!

Adult Help   **Long Time**   **Don't Eat**

Invisible Ink #2

Can secret messages come in colors other than brown? Let's see.

WHAT YOU WILL NEED

Ingredients

- 1 teaspoon (4.9 ml) cornstarch
- 1/2 cup (.12 l) water, divided
- iodine

Equipment

- measuring cups & spoons
- microwave-safe bowl
- spoon
- cotton swab
- white paper
- small bowl
- sponge

1. Place the cornstarch and 1/4 cup (.06 l) water in a microwave-safe bowl and stir.

2. Have an adult microwave the mixture on the high setting for 40 seconds.

3. Stir again, then allow the liquid to cool.

4. Use your "ink" and a cotton swab to write a secret message on a piece of white paper and place it someplace safe to dry.

5. Have an adult put several drops of iodine in a bowl and add the remaining 1/4 cup (.06 l) water. **Iodine is poisonous, so do not taste or drink this liquid.** Dip a sponge in the iodine mixture and lightly wipe the sponge over the dried paper. Can you read your message? What color is it?

6. Make sure you wash your hands with soap and water after you have used the iodine mixture!

Adult Help   Long Time   Don't Eat

Disappearing Ink

Now you see it. Now you don't. Where did that message go?

WHAT YOU WILL NEED

Ingredients

- 1/4 cup (.06 l) water
- iodine
- spray starch

Equipment

- measuring cups
- shallow pan
- cotton swab
- white paper

1. Have an adult put the water and about 5 drops of iodine into a shallow pan. (A pie plate works well.) **Iodine is poisonous, so do not taste or drink this liquid.**

2. You need to do this step in a well-ventilated room or outside. Have an adult squirt spray starch into the pan, holding the nozzle down for about 10 seconds.

3. Dip a cotton swab into the liquid and use it to write a message on a piece of white paper.

4. Watch the paper. Over the next few hours, the message will slowly disappear.

5. Make sure you wash your hands with soap and water after you have used the iodine mixture!

Adult Help   Long Time   Don't Eat

•18•

•PAPER MAKING & PRINTING•

Paper making is a safe and fun activity, but there are two things you should watch out for. Always have an adult help you use the blender, and if it starts to strain or overheat, **TURN IT OFF.** Overloading the blender can damage it. If the blender seems too full, remove some pulp and continue. Also, dispose of the water from the pulp carefully. Don't flush it down the toilet or pour it down the sink; instead, strain out all the solid pulp and put it in the garbage, then dispose of the liquid down the drain.

Recycled Paper

Make your own paper for unique cards and gifts!

WHAT YOU WILL NEED

Ingredients

- 4 cups (.96 l) finely shredded used paper
- warm water

Equipment

- measuring cups
- bucket
- blender
- deep baking dish
- wire coat hanger
- nylon pantyhose

1. Place the paper in a bucket filled with warm water and let it sit until softened, about 1 hour.

2. Have an adult fill a blender halfway with the softened paper and pulse it to break apart the paper fibers. The pulp should look like watery oatmeal. Pour the pulp into a deep baking dish and repeat this step with the remaining paper until all the paper is processed.

3. Have an adult stretch a wire coat hanger into a square and slide it into one leg of a pair of pantyhose to make a screen.

4. Scoop the screen through the pulp mixture to collect some of the pulp. Gently smooth the pulp out across the screen in an even layer. Allow the pulp to dry on the screen overnight. Peel your paper off the screen when it is dry. Dispose of any extra mixture by straining the pulp out of the water. Pour the water down the sink. Place the pulp in a plastic bag and throw it in the garbage.

•19•

Adult Help   Long Time   Don't Eat

Smelly Paper

Don't you love those little stickers in magazines that tell you to scratch and sniff? They can sometimes smell exactly like the flower or fruit in the picture. Wouldn't you like to make your own scratch-and-sniff paper? Well, try this.

WHAT YOU WILL NEED

Ingredients

- 1 teaspoon (4.9 ml) smelly stuff (use one or a mixture of ground cinnamon, cloves, ginger, curry powder, vanilla, cocoa, perfume, or any other scent you'd like)
- paper pulp (from Recycled Paper on p. 19)

1. During step 2 on p. 19, add the smelly stuff to the pulp in the baking dish and mix together. If you don't want all of your paper to be scented, put some of the pulp into another dish and add your smelly stuff.

2. Follow the rest of the instructions on p. 19. Except this time when you're done, you can scratch and sniff!

Adult Help   Long Time   Don't Eat

Food Prints

Your parents probably tell you not to play with your food, but there are exceptions. Remember: Do not eat this food after you have played with it.

WHAT YOU WILL NEED

Equipment

- apple
- knife
- paper towel
- liquid tempera paint
- tray or saucer
- paintbrush
- paper
- other fruits or vegetables
- frozen waffle, defrosted (optional)
- newspaper

1. Have an adult cut the apple in half crosswise. (Notice the tiny star in the middle?) Blot half the fruit with a paper towel to remove the excess juice.

2. Pour some tempera paint into a tray or saucer. With a paintbrush, paint the flat side of the fruit, then press it onto a piece of paper. Carefully peel the paper off the fruit.

3. Try this using different fruits and vegetables. What kinds of patterns do other fruits make?

4. Use a frozen waffle to make a checkered print. Pat the waffle dry and place it on newspaper. Then use a paintbrush to cover one side of the waffle with different colors of paint. Place a piece of paper over the waffle and use your hands to press the paper down evenly over the paint. Carefully peel your paper off the waffle.

Adult Help

Don't Eat

Spider Prints

Want to make a cool picture with the help of some spider friends? No, you aren't going to take a print from the hairy legs of an arachnid! Gross.

WHAT YOU WILL NEED

Equipment

- spider's web
- talcum powder (optional)
- pump hairspray
- black construction paper
- nerves of steel!

1. Find a pretty spider's web. Look for one that does not have a spider perched on it. Abandoned webs work best. If you'd like, you can sprinkle talcum powder on the web to make your print stand out more.

2. Spray both sides of the web with hairspray.

3. You'll have to be fast—place a piece of black construction paper on the web before the hairspray dries.

4. Use your nerves of steel to break off the edges of the web and release it from whatever it is attached to. Run like crazy away from the web. (Just kidding!)

5. Mount the picture and display it proudly.

Adult Help

Don't Eat

•22•

Eyd Eit (Backward Tie Dye)

Tie-dyed clothes look really terrific, but we always forget to buy dye. Here is a way to make your old, stained, or tired clothes look new, no dye needed! Make sure to wear old clothes while doing this project—you don't want to accidentally dye your good clothes!

WHAT YOU WILL NEED

Equipment

- a solid-colored, 100% cotton T-shirt or other article of clothing
- rubber bands
- plastic bucket
- laundry bleach
- rubber gloves

1. Scrunch together different parts of the T-shirt and wrap rubber bands around the sections tightly. Do this several times until you have lots of rubber bands attached.

2. In a well-ventilated area, have an adult fill a plastic bucket halfway with bleach, then put on rubber gloves and submerge the T-shirt.

3. Leave the T-shirt in the bleach for 20 to 30 minutes.

4. Have an adult rinse the T-shirt thoroughly to remove the bleach. Then take off the rubber bands and launder the T-shirt.

5. Try it on! Now you have a shirt that is happening!

•23•

Adult Help

Long Time

Don't Eat

•SLIMES•

This may be the most fun part of the book.
But there are important things to know before making slime:

• Never eat, taste, or drink any of the liquids or guck. • Do not flush slimes down the toilet or pour down drains. Toss them away in sealed bags. • Only adults should handle borax and borax solutions. Some people are allergic to borax. If you have sensitive skin, wear gloves. • These activities can be messy. Cover your work and play areas with newspaper before you begin. • Always wash your hands with soap and water after playing with slimes.• Slimes can be harmful and can damage many surfaces. Don't put slime on wood tables. Don't throw it on walls, carpets, or drapes. Don't leave slime in your back pocket when you put your pants in the wash! • Keep slimes away from small children and animals.

Suspended Slime

This slime doesn't know what it wants to be: a solid or a liquid. What do you think?

WHAT YOU WILL NEED

Ingredients

- 1 cup (.24 l) cornstarch
- food coloring
- 1/2 to 3/4 cup (.12 to .18 l) water

Equipment

- measuring cups
- large bowl

1. Place the cornstarch in a large bowl and add a few drops of food coloring.

2. Add the water a little bit at a time. Use your hand to mix this mess. Do not add too much water all at once or else you will get milky, watery goop.

3. You know you have enough water when the cornstarch holds together.

4. Gather a blob in your hand and watch it ooze out between your fingertips.

5. Punch the blob and it forms a solid surface.

6. When you are finished playing, place the slime in a plastic bag, seal it, and put it in the garbage. You can also dry your slime by spreading it out on a piece of wax paper and letting it air-dry. Add water when you want to play with it again.

•24•

Adult Help

Don't Eat

Bouncing Slimy Putty

Here's a simple way to make a runny, plastic gob.

What You Will Need

Ingredients

- 1/2 cup (.12 l) white glue
- food coloring
- hand cream or glycerine (Vaseline® Intensive Care works best)
- 3/4 cup (.18 l) warm water
- 1 tablespoon (14.8 ml) borax

Equipment

- measuring cups & spoons
- 2 resealable plastic bags

1. Pour the glue into a plastic bag. Add a drop of food coloring and a tiny squirt of hand cream or glycerine. Don't add too much cream or else the slime won't hold together! Seal the bag, then squeeze the goo to mix.

2. Put the warm water into a second bag and have an adult add the borax. Seal the bag and shake to mix.

3. Pour about 2 tablespoons (29.6 ml) of the borax mixture into the bag of goo. Close the bag and mush between your fingers.

4. Pour the rest of the borax liquid into the bag of goo. Seal the bag and knead until you have a solid gob. Now it's ready to take out and play with!

5. Drain the excess water surrounding the gob. Wash your hands with soap and water. Store the gob in the plastic bag after you are finished playing.

Adult Help

Don't Eat

Electric Slime

Watch out for this slime. It's ALIVE!

WHAT YOU WILL NEED

Ingredients

- 3/4 cup (.18 l) cornstarch
- 2 cups (.48 l) vegetable oil

Equipment

- measuring cups
- jar with lid
- spoon
- Styrofoam
- silk or wool scarf or other article of clothing

1. Pour the cornstarch and oil into a jar, cover, and shake to mix.

2. Leave this in the fridge for several hours, until it is cold.

3. Remove from the fridge, uncover, and use a spoon to mix. Hold the jar in your hot little hands to warm the mixture.

4. Build up a charge on the Styrofoam by rubbing it on a piece of silk or wool. (Anything made out of Styrofoam will work, including packaging material or even a Styrofoam cup.)

5. Have a helper turn the jar sideways so the liquid begins to ooze out of the mouth of the jar.

6. Hold the charged Styrofoam in the path of the ooze. The ooze should come to a halt.

7. Recharge the Styrofoam and see if the ooze will follow the Styrofoam along the counter. Scoop up the slime and try this again. Store your slime in a plastic bag when you are finished playing.

Adult Help   **Long Time**   **Don't Eat**

•26•

Mutant Slime

You don't need to be a superhero to win a fight with this slime.

What You Will Need

Ingredients

- 1/2 cup (.12 l) clear gel glue (Elmer's® makes a good one)
- food coloring
- 3/4 cup (.18 l) warm water
- 1 tablespoon (14.8 ml) borax

Equipment

- measuring cups & spoons
- 2 large resealable plastic bags

1. Pour the glue into a plastic bag and add a drop of food coloring.

2. Put the warm water into a second bag and have an adult add the borax. Seal the bag and shake to mix.

3. Pour about 2 tablespoons (29.6 ml) of the borax mixture into the colored goop. Seal the bag and squeeze it between your fingers.

4. Pour the rest of the borax liquid into the goop. Close the bag and knead until the mixture holds together. Now it's ready to play with!

5. Drain the excess borax mixture surrounding the slime. Wash your hands with soap and water. Store your slime in the plastic bag after you are finished playing.

Adult Help

Don't Eat

Udderly Gross Slime

What do cows and slime have in common? You'd be surprised.

WHAT YOU WILL NEED

Ingredients

- 1/2 cup (.12 l) milk
- 1 tablespoon (14.8 ml) vinegar
- 1 teaspoon (4.9 ml) water (optional)
- 1 teaspoon (4.9 ml) baking soda (optional)

Equipment

- measuring cups & spoons
- saucepan
- spoon
- strainer
- small container with lid

1. Combine the milk and vinegar in a saucepan. Have an adult warm the mixture over medium heat until small lumps form.

2. After the adult removes the saucepan from the stove, stir the guck until you get white lumps in clear liquid.

3. Strain the lumps and discard the liquid. You've got a new kind of slime! To store the slime for later use, put it in a sealed container in the fridge.

4. If you want to make glue with the slime, simply add 1 teaspoon (4.9 ml) of water and 1 teaspoon (4.9 ml) of baking soda to the lumps and stir.

Adult Help

Don't Eat

Victual Slime

"Victual" is what is known as a "five dollar," or fancy, word for food. This is one of the few times it will be okay for you to taste an activity!

WHAT YOU WILL NEED

Ingredients

- 1/2 cup (.12 l) cornstarch
- 1/4 cup (.06 l) corn syrup
- several drops of food coloring
- 1 teaspoon (4.9 ml) water
- chopped gummy candy (optional)

Equipment

- measuring cups & spoons
- bowl
- spoon
- container with lid

1. Put the cornstarch, corn syrup, food coloring, and water into a bowl.

2. Mix with a spoon to form a paste. You may add a little extra cornstarch if the mixture is too wet or a little more syrup if it is too dry. Add chopped-up candies to make the mixture look like edible barf. Eat right away, or store in a sealed container in the fridge.

Adult Help

Miss Muffet Slime

Remember little Miss Muffet? She sat on her tuffet, eating her curds and whey. While we can only guess what a tuffet is, we definitely know what curds are, and we know they make great slime!

WHAT YOU WILL NEED

Ingredients

- 1 cup (.24 l) skim milk
- 2 tablespoons (29.6 ml) vinegar
- 1 teaspoon (4.9 ml) borax
- 3 tablespoons (44 ml) warm water

Equipment

- measuring cups & spoons
- microwave-safe bowl
- strainer
- small cup
- resealable plastic bag

1. Have an adult warm the skim milk in a bowl in the microwave, then add the vinegar to the milk. It will look vile as small lumps form in a yucky liquid. Strain the curds (lumps) and discard the liquid. Rinse off the curds in a strainer under a faucet.

2. Have an adult place the borax and warm water in a small cup. Allow the borax to dissolve.

3. Drop the curds into the borax liquid and let the mixture sit until a smooth paste forms. This should take only a few minutes. It's a slime! Wash your hands with soap and water when you're done playing. Store in a sealed plastic bag in the refrigerator for up to two weeks.

Adult Help

Don't Eat

•30•

Psylly Slime

Want to make the coolest slime? Here's one that looks just like the store-bought variety!

WHAT YOU WILL NEED

Ingredients

- 1 teaspoon (4.9 ml) Metamucil® or psyllium husk (from a health food store)
- 1 1/4 cups (.30 l) water
- food coloring

Equipment

- measuring cups & spoons
- jar with lid
- large glass microwave-safe container
- resealable plastic bag

1. Combine the Metamucil® or psyllium and water in a jar. Tightly seal the jar and shake it like crazy for a few minutes.

2. Pour the guck into a glass, microwave-safe container and add a few drops of green or blue food coloring.

3. Put the container in the microwave.

4. Have an adult set the microwave on high for three minutes. Press STOP when the liquid begins to ooze out of the container. Do not remove from the microwave!

5. Wait three minutes, then microwave for five minutes more. Have an adult remove the container. Wait an hour before you play with the slime or else you will burn your fingers. When you're done playing, store the slime in a resealable plastic bag so it doesn't dry out.

Adult Help   Long Time   Don't Eat

•COLOR CHANGES•

While cabbage and some of the other ingredients used in this section are edible, don't eat, drink, or taste these experiments. In fact, you should never eat any strange mixtures without first asking a responsible adult.

Red Cabbage Concoction

The next few projects all start with a red cabbage soup. This is the master recipe you need!

WHAT YOU WILL NEED

Ingredients

- 3 cups (.72 l) sliced red cabbage
- 3 cups (.72 l) boiling water

Equipment

- measuring cups
- 2 large heat-proof bowls
- strainer
- covered storage container

1. Place the sliced cabbage in a heat-proof bowl. Have an adult pour the boiling water over the top of the cabbage.

2. Let the cabbage sit in the water until it is cool. This should take about 10 minutes.

3. Place a strainer over a second bowl. Pour the cabbage mixture into the strainer, collecting the cabbage juice in the second bowl.

4. Store the strained cabbage juice in a covered container. (Place it in the fridge if you are going to keep it for longer than one day.) Throw out the cooked cabbage.

WHAT'S GOING ON...

Cabbage juice contains a chemical that has two forms, each with a different color. When the juice is mixed with other chemicals called *acids*, you see one form of the cabbage chemical: red. When the juice is mixed with chemicals called *bases*, you see the other form of the cabbage chemical: blue. Sometimes you can see both forms of the cabbage chemical and the mixture looks purple.

Adult Help

Don't Eat

•32•

Am I Blue?

Your cabbage concoction is amazing stuff; not only is it red, but sometimes it can be blue! Here is a way to make the juice change colors before your very eyes. Have an adult help you handle the ammonia and vinegar—it can hurt if these substances get in a cut or in your eyes.

What You Will Need

Ingredients

- 1/2 cup (.12 l) Red Cabbage Concoction, divided (see p. 32)
- 3 tablespoons (44 ml) ammonia, divided
- 3 tablespoons (44 ml) white or cider vinegar, divided

Equipment

- measuring cups & spoons
- 2 drinking glasses

1. Place 1/4 cup (.06 l) of the cabbage concoction into each of two drinking glasses.

2. Add a tablespoon (14.8 ml) of ammonia to the concoction in one of the glasses. Look at the mixture to see its color.

3. Add a tablespoon (14.8 ml) of vinegar to the concoction in the other glass. What color is this mixture?

4. Now add 2 tablespoons (29.6 ml) of ammonia to the glass containing the vinegar and cabbage concoction. What happens? What happens if you add 2 tablespoons (29.6 ml) of vinegar to the glass containing the ammonia and cabbage mixture?

5. Pour both mixtures down the drain and wash the glasses well when your experiment is completed.

•33•

Adult Help   Don't Eat

Quick-Change Paper

Scientists use something called a *litmus test* to determine if the chemicals they are working with are acids or bases. Sometimes they use special paper, called *litmus paper*, to perform this test. Litmus paper turns red when dipped in acids, and it turns blue when placed in a base. Here is an easy way to make your own litmus paper.

1. Pour enough cabbage concoction into a shallow dish or tray so that there is a layer about 1/4-inch (.6-cm) deep.

2. Place the coffee filters in the dish so that each filter is completely covered in cabbage juice. (You can ask an adult to cut the filters into smaller pieces to fit into the dish if you need to.) Leave the filters in the juice for about 10 minutes.

3. Remove the filters from the dish and let them dry. Have an adult cut the filters into 1/2-inch-wide (1.3-cm) strips.

4. Test the strips by dipping some of them into the vinegar and others into the baking soda mixed with the water. What color do the strips become when placed in vinegar? Is vinegar an acid or a base? How about the baking soda? Try dipping the strips into other household liquids. Throw the strips away when you are done with your experiment.

Adult Help   Long Time   Don't Eat

Technicolor Foam

It foams, it fizzes—and it changes color! What more could you ask for?

WHAT YOU WILL NEED

Ingredients

- 1 cup (.24 l) Red Cabbage Concoction (see p. 32)
- 1/2 cup (.12 l) baking soda
- 1 cup (.24 l) vinegar

Equipment

- measuring cups
- deep bowl or large straight-sided vase
- spoon

1. Pour the cabbage juice into the bottom of a deep bowl or a large, straight-sided vase. Your container should be very large or it may overflow. In fact, you should work in the sink, just in case. This can be messy!

2. Mix in the baking soda until it all dissolves.

3. Have an adult slowly pour in the vinegar. Be sure to slow down when it looks like the mixture will spill over. Cool, huh?

4. When you are finished, rinse the whole mixture down the sink with lots of water.

Adult Help

Don't Eat

Hard Rock Candy

If you do this in a clean mug and cover it with wax paper, it is safe to eat the crystals when you are finished. Ask an adult for help and keep everything clean.

WHAT YOU WILL NEED

Ingredients

- 1/4 cup (.06 l) water
- 1/2 cup (.12 l) sugar
- food coloring
- warm water

Equipment

- measuring cups
- small saucepan
- coffee mug
- spoon
- fine fishing line
- pencil
- paper clip (optional)

Adult Help   Long Time

1. Have an adult boil the 1/4 cup (.06 l) water for you, then put it in a coffee mug. Add the sugar and a few drops of food coloring, and mix until most of the sugar dissolves (there will still be a few tablespoons left on the bottom of the mug). Let the water cool. Don't touch the mug until crystals begin to form. (This can take a week or more, depending on room temperature, humidity, and the hardness of the water.)

2. Carefully remove a crystal from the mug. Add a few drops of warm water to the mixture in the mug. Stir to redissolve the remaining crystals.

3. Carefully tie one end of a piece of fishing line to the crystal and the other end to a pencil. Use the pencil and line to suspend the crystal in the sugar water in the mug; it shouldn't touch the sides or bottom. Leave the crystal for a few days and watch it grow!

Hint: If you are having a hard time growing crystals, try attaching a clean paper clip to the fishing line and suspending the paper clip in the water. You may have better luck getting the crystals to form around the paper clip.

Cube It

You may not be able to make your own diamonds, but you can make some cool crystals. Don't eat these!

What You Will Need

Ingredients

- 1/4 cup (.06 l) water
- 1/2 cup (.12 l) alum or table salt
- warm water

Equipment

- measuring cups & spoons
- small saucepan
- coffee mug
- spoon
- straight-sided dish
- fine fishing line
- pencil

1. Have an adult boil the 1/4 cup (.06 l) water for you, then put it in a coffee mug. Add the alum or salt 1 teaspoon (4.9 ml) at a time, mixing to dissolve it completely. Continue to add the alum or salt until no more will dissolve.

2. Let the water cool. When it is cool, pour some into a straight-sided dish so that there is a layer 1/2-inch (1.3-cm) deep. Leave it undisturbed until crystals begin to form. (This can take a week or more, depending on room temperature, humidity, and the hardness of the water.)

3. Carefully remove a crystal from the dish. Pour any leftover mixture back into the coffee mug, add a few drops of warm water, and stir to dissolve all the crystals.

4. Carefully tie one end of a piece of fishing line to the crystal and the other end to a pencil. Use the pencil and line to suspend the crystal in the water in the mug; it shouldn't touch the sides or bottom. Leave the crystal for a few days and watch it grow!

Hint: If you are having a hard time growing crystals, try attaching a paper clip to the fishing line and suspending the paper clip in water. You may have better luck getting the crystals to form around the paper clip.

Long Time

Don't Eat

Crystal Art

Paint a picture, then watch it change into a delicate crystal creation.

1. Place the salt in a small container and pour in the warm water. Stir until most of the salt dissolves.

2. Use a paintbrush and the saltwater mixture to create secret messages or unusual pictures on black construction paper.

3. Have an adult turn on the oven to 150° Fahrenheit (66° Celsius)—this is usually the "warm" setting—and no higher.

4. When you have finished your masterpiece, have the adult place the picture on an oven rack and bake for five minutes. You'll know the picture is "cooked" when white, shiny crystals appear on the paper. Remove the paper from the oven immediately.

Adult Help

Don't Eat

·38·

These next activities involve eggs. While eggs seem pretty harmless, you can get nasty bugs from handling raw ones. Make sure you wash your hands and all utensils and surfaces after using eggs. Don't eat any of the eggs you use in these experiments!

Secret Egg Messages

Can an egg read your mind? Let's see.

WHAT YOU WILL NEED

Ingredients

- 1 tablespoon (14.8 ml) vinegar
- 1 teaspoon (4.9 ml) alum
- hard-boiled white egg in its shell at room temperature

Equipment

- measuring spoons
- small plastic container
- spoon
- paper & pen
- cotton swab or paintbrush

1. Place the vinegar and the alum in a small plastic container, and stir to dissolve the alum.

2. Think of a question to ask your sibling or parent at the breakfast table, something simple, such as, "What's our phone number?" Write the question on a piece of paper using a pen. Write the answer on the outside of the eggshell using the vinegar and alum mixture and a cotton swab or paintbrush.

3. Place the egg someplace safe to dry (not in the fridge).

4. Wait a day or so before doing your trick. Tell your family you have a magical egg. Hand a family member the piece of paper with the question written on it and ask him or her to read it out loud.

5. Gently peel the shell off the egg to reveal the answer.

Adult Help   Long Time   Don't Eat

Invisible Eggs

Now you know that eggs can read minds, but did you know their shells can also disappear?

WHAT YOU WILL NEED

Ingredients

- a hard-boiled egg and a raw egg (white eggs work best) in their shells
- white vinegar

Equipment

- crayon
- 2 glass jars (lids optional)

1. Using a crayon, draw funny faces on the eggshells.

2. Gently place the hard-boiled egg in a jar and cover the egg with vinegar. Do the same thing with the uncooked egg in a second jar. Leave the jars on a counter overnight. (You can cover the jars if you wish, to cut down on the vinegar smell; it shouldn't really slow things down much.)

3. The next day, have an adult gently pour out the old vinegar from the jars and replace it with fresh vinegar. Let the jars sit for two weeks without touching or moving them.

4. After two weeks, remove the eggs from the jars and rinse the eggs under cold water. Pour the vinegar down the drain. Gently drop each egg on the floor. No, don't slam-dunk them! The eggs should bounce. What do you see when the shells dissolve?

Adult Help   Long Time   Don't Eat

•40•

Vanishing Eggs

This is a really cool variation of the **INVISIBLE EGGS** activity.

WHAT YOU WILL NEED

Ingredients

- an extra-large raw white egg in its shell
- white vinegar
- talcum powder

Equipment

- pin
- glass jar (lid optional)

1. Carefully wash the eggshell with soap and water. Use a pin to poke a small hole in both ends of the egg. (An adult may need to help you with this step.)

2. Have an adult blow out the insides of the egg.

3. Gently place the hollowed eggshell in a jar filled with vinegar. It will float. Leave the jar on a counter for up to two weeks. (You can cover the jar if you wish, to cut down on the vinegar smell.)

4. When the eggshell starts to look rubbery, remove the egg from the vinegar. Pour the vinegar down the drain. Rinse the egg, dry it, and dust it with talcum powder.

5. Your egg can be squished flat, and it will return to its oval shape. Create your own magic trick by squeezing the egg between your fingers to make it disappear.

Adult Help   Long Time   Don't Eat

Egg Pets

Save an eggshell from the compost heap and turn it into a furry pet. Here's a creature you won't have to take for walks.

WHAT YOU WILL NEED

Ingredients

- soft-boiled egg in its shell
- tiny pebbles
- potting soil
- grass or other seeds (such as alfalfa)
- water

Equipment

- knife
- spoon
- felt pens or paints
- egg carton

1. Have an adult carefully cut the top quarter from a soft-boiled egg. Gently rinse out all the guck inside the eggshell.

2. Spoon a few tiny pebbles into the bottom of the shell, then cover the pebbles with loose potting soil.

3. Cover the soil with a dusting of grass seed or other similar seed and lightly wet the soil. Create a face on your egg with paints or felt pens.

4. Put the egg back into its carton and place in a sunny window. Keep the soil moist.

5. Trim the "hair" as it grows. (You won't begin to see anything for several days.)

6. Try growing another egg buddy, but use cotton balls instead of soil.

Adult Help   Long Time   Don't Eat

Egg Floats

This silly trick will keep you busy *and* amuse your friends.

WHAT YOU WILL NEED

Ingredients

- 2 cups (.48 l) hot water
- salt
- cold water
- raw egg in its shell

Equipment

- measuring cups
- 3 large glass jars
- long spoon

1. Have an adult place the hot water in a jar. Slowly add salt to the water while stirring. When a layer of salt forms on the bottom of the jar, you've got enough salt.

2. Fill another jar with cold water and gently place the egg in the jar using a long spoon. It goes to the bottom of the jar. Big deal.

3. Remove the egg. Use your spoon to place the egg in the jar with the salt water. Did the egg sink?

4. Have an adult pour half the salt water into a third jar. Slowly spoon cold, fresh water over the salty water. Don't mix! Use your spoon to place the egg into this water. Where is the egg now?

Adult Help

Don't Eat

•YEAST—IT'LL GROW ON YOU•

Yeast is wonderful stuff—and it's alive! Give it a little bit of warm water and sugar to eat and it grows and grows! Yeast is not a plant or an animal, it is a *fungus*, like a mushroom. It grows faster than plants and is less messy than any type of pet.

A Fungus Among Us

WHAT YOU WILL NEED

Ingredients

- 1 cup (.24 l) warm water
- 1 teaspoon (4.9 ml) sugar
- 1 package instant dry yeast

Equipment

- measuring cups & spoons
- large bowl
- spoon

If you've never worked with yeast before, this is the activity for you! (And you are on your way to making a delicious homemade pizza! See the next page...)

1. Place the warm water in a bowl. Note: The water should be warm enough to make the yeast grow but not too hot to touch.

2. Stir in the sugar so that it dissolves completely.

3. Add the yeast, then stir the mixture. Watch it for about 10 minutes to see what happens. Your yeast should grow about one-third in size. If your mixture doesn't bubble and swell up, check the yeast package to make sure it was fresh!

4. Once the yeast has grown, use it right away in the pizza recipe on the next page.

Adult Help

Perfect Pizza

Once you have made yeast grow, you've almost made pizza! Here are the rest of the instructions (add other toppings besides cheese and tomato sauce if you'd like).

WHAT YOU WILL NEED

Ingredients

- yeast mixture (see p. 44)
- 2 1/2 cups (.60 l) flour
- 1/2 teaspoon (2.5 ml) salt
- 1 8-oz. (.24-l) can tomato or pizza sauce
- 1 cup (.24 l) grated mozzarella cheese

Equipment

- measuring cups & spoons
- greased bowl
- dishcloth or plastic wrap
- greased cookie sheet

1. Add the flour and salt to your warm yeast mixture and stir until a dough forms. Knead the dough by pushing it down and away from you and folding it over until it is shiny. (If the mixture is too sticky, add a little more flour.) Place the dough in a greased bowl and cover it with a dishcloth or plastic wrap. Leave it in a warm place until it doubles in size. This should take from 40 minutes to an hour.

2. Use the heel of your hand to flatten the dough out on a greased cookie sheet. Turn up the edges to hold in the sauce. Make the dough as thick or as thin as you'd like your crust.

3. Cover the dough with a thin layer of sauce and all of the grated mozzarella cheese. Have an adult bake the pizza in a 425° Fahrenheit (220° Celsius) oven for 10 minutes, or until brown around the edges. You can eat this yummy concoction!

Adult Help   Long Time

Automatic Balloon

This is the perfect thing to do on a rainy afternoon when you don't feel like doing anything!

WHAT YOU WILL NEED

Ingredients

- 1 package instant dry yeast
- 1 teaspoon (4.9 ml) sugar
- 1 cup (.24 l) warm water

Equipment

- measuring cups & spoons
- funnel
- round balloon

1. Place the bottom of a funnel into the mouth of a balloon and hold it in position.

2. Pour the yeast and sugar into the balloon through the funnel.

3. Pour the warm water slowly down the side of the funnel so that it goes into the balloon. If you pour too fast, it might not go in, so take it nice and slow. **If the balloon breaks, throw it out immediately and use another one.**

4. Remove the funnel from the neck of the balloon. Tie a knot in the neck of the balloon to seal it. Place the balloon in a warm place and watch it blow up! The balloon will stay inflated for a day or two. Throw it in the garbage when you're finished with it.

Adult Help

Don't Eat

Shrunken Heads

In old adventure movies, hostile locals sometimes have shrunken "heads" hanging from their belts. Here's a nicer way to create the same illusion.

WHAT YOU WILL NEED

Ingredients

- large, firm apple, with stem, without bruises
- lemon juice (fresh or from concentrate)

Equipment

- small knife
- bowl
- string
- coat hanger

1. Have an adult peel the apple, leaving a 1-inch (2.5-cm) rim of peel around the stem. Don't remove the stem.

2. Work with an adult to carve a face into the apple. Keep it simple.

3. Place the apple in a bowl and add lemon juice until the apple is covered. Let it sit for an hour.

4. Tie a piece of string to the stem, and tie the other end of the string to a coat hanger. Hang in a garage or other enclosed outdoor area for a few weeks, until the apple is dried up and shriveled.

5. Decorate your "head"—you can add feathers, eyes, or other scary things—and display on your belt or anywhere you like!

Adult Help **Long Time** **Don't Eat**

Bee-you-tee-ful

WHAT YOU WILL NEED

Ingredients

- 1 tablespoon (14.8 ml) grated beeswax
- water
- 2 teaspoons (9.9 ml) mineral oil
- 1/4 teaspoon (1.2 ml) peppermint extract

Equipment

- measuring spoons
- heat-proof measuring cup
- heat-proof bowl
- spoon
- 6-inch (15.24-cm) square of aluminum foil or a small plastic or metal container

It takes only a little bit of beeswax to keep your lips smooth and soft in summer or winter. Keep this lip balm handy to help prevent chapped lips.

1. Place the beeswax in a heat-proof measuring cup. Put the measuring cup into a heat-proof bowl. Have an adult boil water and add it to the bowl (around the cup) so the level of the water is above the height of the wax in the cup.

2. Stir the wax gently with a spoon until all the wax has melted. Slowly add the mineral oil and peppermint extract to the wax and continue mixing until they are blended together.

3. Pinch up the sides of a piece of aluminum foil to make a small bowl, or use a small plastic or metal container. Pour the melted wax mixture into the foil or other container. Allow the wax mixture to sit for a few minutes to cool and harden. Use your finger to apply the lip balm to your lips.

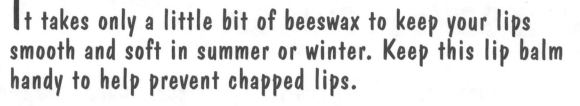

Adult Help

Jelly Plastic

Look around you. How many things do you see that are made from plastic? Think you can make your own plastic? Try this.

1. Place the gelatin in a small bowl. Have an adult boil the water. Spoon 3 tablespoons (44 ml) of boiling water into the gelatin. Stir until the gelatin is completely dissolved.

2. Divide the dissolved gelatin evenly among 5 plastic lids. Add a drop of food coloring to each lid and stir gently, or let the color sit and see what happens.

3. Leave the lids on the counter for several days, until the "plastic" is dry and hardened.

4. Pop the plastic from the lids. An adult can help you cut the plastic into interesting shapes and designs.

Adult Help   Long Time   Don't Eat

Jelly Snakes

These slippery concoctions look like mutant reptiles. Best of all, you can eat them!

What You Will Need

Ingredients

- 1 envelope unflavored gelatin
- 2/3 cup (.16 l) colored juice

Equipment

- measuring cups
- small bowl
- small saucepan
- spoon
- loaf tin
- 8 to 10 plastic drinking straws

1. Place the gelatin in a small bowl. Have an adult boil the juice and add it to the gelatin, a little at a time. Stir until all the gelatin powder has dissolved.

2. Allow the liquid to cool to room temperature, then pour into a loaf tin.

3. Lay the straws flat in the loaf tin. You may have to have an adult cut the straws to get them to fit. Make sure the straws are submerged in the liquid.

4. Put the loaf tin in the fridge for several hours.

5. When the gelatin has set, pick up the straws and squeeze out the "snakes" by gently pressing from one end.

Adult Help   Long Time

Rubber Bones

Do chickens have rubber bones? Let's see.

WHAT YOU WILL NEED

Ingredients

- a chicken bone from a cooked chicken
- white vinegar

Equipment

- jar with a lid

1. Have an adult supervise as you clean the meat, stringy stuff, and white cartilage from a chicken bone. It must be really clean before you start!

2. Place the bone in a jar and cover with vinegar. Tightly close the jar and set aside for about a week.

3. Remove the bone from the vinegar and rinse in water. See if you can bend the bone into a shape. If you can't, put fresh vinegar in the jar and leave for another day. The vinegar can be poured down the drain when you're finished with it.

Adult Help   Long Time   Don't Eat

Bottle Currents

This liquid looks like something from outer space, but you can use it to wash your hands.

WHAT YOU WILL NEED

Ingredients

- liquid hand soap that contains glycol stearate (Softsoap® is perfect)
- food coloring (optional)
- water

Equipment

- clear, 16-ounce (473-ml) plastic bottle and cap

1. Fill the bottle about one quarter of the way full with the liquid soap. Add a few drops of food coloring if you wish (not too much or else you will ruin the effect).

2. Slowly fill the bottle to the rim with water. If you have bubbles or foam at the top, add more water until the bubbles are out of the bottle.

3. Tightly screw on the cap and turn the bottle upside down several times. What do you see?

4. Swirl and shake the bottle and watch the soapy eddies in the container.

Adult Help

Don't Eat

Fizzy Bubble-Bath Balls

These are the most amazing concoctions to put into a bathtub. They bubble and fizz and leave your skin feeling soft and smooth.

What You Will Need

Ingredients

- 1/3 cup (.08 l) citric acid
- 1 cup (.24 l) baking soda
- witch hazel (available at drugstores)

Equipment

- measuring cups
- mixing bowl
- spoon
- pump spray bottle
- plastic bag

1. Place the citric acid and the baking soda in a bowl and stir to mix.

2. Pour some witch hazel into the spray bottle and screw the top on tightly.

3. Spray a small amount of witch hazel into the acid-soda mixture. Mix well. Repeat until the acid-soda mixture clumps together when squeezed in your hands. Don't let the mixture get too wet.

4. Put the mixture into a plastic bag and squeeze it into a few small balls. Leave the bag open to allow the balls to dry. Once they are dry, you can add them to your water when you take a bath.

•53•

Adult Help   Long Time   Don't Eat

Rainbow Bath Salts

These bath salts make wonderful, colorful gifts. The multicolored layers of glistening salt look particularly good in clear glass bottles. For people with sensitive skin you can leave out the perfume or essential oils.

What You Will Need

Ingredients

- Epsom salts
- perfume or essential oils (oils can be found in a health food store)
- food coloring

Equipment

- measuring cups
- disposable plastic containers—1-pound (.45-kg) margarine or butter tubs work well
- spoons
- clear glass jars or plastic containers with lids

1. For each color you are making, place 1 cup (.24 l) of Epsom salts in a disposable plastic container and add a drop or two of perfume or essential oil. Add food coloring while stirring the salts until the salts reach the desired color.

2. Place a layer of the first color into a glass jar or plastic container, then add a layer of the next color on top, then the third, and so on. Keep adding layers until you have created a pattern you like. Put the lid on the container and seal tightly until you are ready to add the salts to your bath water. Fill as many clear containers as you want!

3. Add 1 to 2 tablespoons (14.8 to 29.6 ml) to your next bath!

Adult Help

Don't Eat

Beautiful Bath Oil

Pretty clear glass or plastic containers decorate any bathroom and look particularly nice when filled with colored bath oils. Here is an easy, inexpensive way to make your own luxurious oil.

WHAT YOU WILL NEED

Ingredients

- 1 cup (.24 l) baby oil
- perfume or essential oil
- powdered food coloring

Equipment

- measuring cups
- clear glass jar or plastic container with lid
- spoon

1. Pour the baby oil into the glass jar or plastic container. Add a drop or two of your favorite perfume or essential oil.

2. Add food coloring a little bit at a time until the oil is the desired color. Put the lid on the container and shake well after each addition. Try a mixture of colors— yellow and blue to make green, or red and blue to make purple.

3. Seal the container tightly and store until you are ready to use the oil in the bath. Add 1 to 2 tablespoons (14.8 ml to 29.6 ml) to your water.

Adult Help

Don't Eat

Creamy Ice

Here's a cool treat for a hot day. When making food products, it's always a good idea for an adult to supervise.

What You Will Need

Ingredients

- 1 cup (.24 l) heavy cream
- 1/2 cup (.12 l) chocolate milk
- 1 teaspoon (4.9 ml) vanilla
- 1/2 cup (.12 l) sugar
- crushed ice
- rock salt

Equipment

- measuring cups & spoons
- clean 1-pound (.45-kg) coffee can with plastic lid
- large pail
- spoon

1. Pour the cream, chocolate milk, vanilla, and sugar into the coffee can. Put the lid on the can and shake for about a minute. Place in the freezer for about 30 minutes.

2. Fill a large pail halfway with crushed ice, and sprinkle rock salt on the ice. Take the can from the freezer and wedge it into this ice.

3. Cover the entire coffee can with crushed ice and salt. Make sure the lid is on tightly or else you will get salty ice cream.

4. Let sit for 10 minutes. Remove the can from the ice, take off the lid, scrape down the sides of the can, and stir with a spoon. Put the lid back on and let sit in the ice and salt for another 5 minutes. Open and stir again. Keep doing this until the mixture looks slushy. When the concoction is ready, eat and enjoy!

Adult Help   Long Time

•56•

Swirling Lava

Remember the '60s? Of course you don't! But thanks to a wave of nostalgia, you can make a replica of this cool lamp that was totally hot thirty-five years ago!

WHAT YOU WILL NEED

Ingredients

- different kinds of oils (such as vegetable, olive, corn, baby)
- food coloring
- ice cube

Equipment

- measuring cups
- 12-ounce (340-g) glass jar with lid (a tall jam or olive jar works best)
- funnel

1. Pour about 1/4 cup (.06 l) of each oil into the jar. It doesn't matter in which order you add the oils.

2. Add a few drops of food coloring. Place the funnel over the glass container so the thin end just touches the top of the oil.

3. Drop an ice cube into the funnel and watch the oil as the ice cube melts.

4. After the ice has melted, remove the funnel and tightly close the lid on the jar. Turn the jar upside down and see what happens to the oils.

·57·

Adult Help

Don't Eat

Soy Divers

Do you think you can get a fast-food packet of soy sauce to perform a trick? This next activity looks really silly, but it's lots of fun!

What You Will Need

Ingredients

- water
- several foil or plastic packages of soy sauce

Equipment

- large clear plastic soda bottle with cap

1. Fill a sink halfway with water and toss in all the soy packets. Look for one that is neither floating on top of the water nor sinking to the bottom of the sink.

2. Fill a plastic soda bottle to the top with water, then pour out about 1/2 cup (.12 l) of water.

3. Stuff a few of the soy packets into the bottle, then cap tightly. Make sure the one floating in the middle of the sink is in the bottle too!

4. Squeeze the bottle really hard (you might need an adult to help you with this part), and watch what happens to the soy packets.

5. Try this with other kinds of fast-food packets, such as mustard or ketchup.

Adult Help

Don't Eat

•58•

Alien Acid

Have you ever noticed how alien blood always foams in movies? Here's how it's done.

WHAT YOU WILL NEED

Ingredients

- 1 tablespoon (14.8 ml) baking soda
- 1 tablespoon (14.8 ml) corn syrup
- food coloring
- 1 teaspoon (4.9 ml) white vinegar

Equipment

- measuring spoons
- bowl
- spoon
- eyedropper

1. Place the baking soda and corn syrup and several drops of food coloring in a bowl and stir until the mixture forms a smooth paste. This paste is your alien blood.

2. Make sure that you're wearing old clothes! This can get messy and may stain fabrics. Drizzle a bit of paste onto your body. Make sure you keep the mixture away from your eyes, your head, or any part of your body that has a cut.

3. Do this step over a sink or bathtub, or, preferably, outdoors. Fill the eyedropper with vinegar. Drip the vinegar onto the paste and watch that blood foam up!

•59•

Adult Help

Don't Eat

Mouth Volcano

Here are two ways to gross out your friends and family. A word of warning, though (actually, several words of warning, if you want to be exact): Don't swallow this stuff. It won't harm you, but it tastes really bad.

WHAT YOU WILL NEED

Ingredients#1

- 5 tablespoons (74 ml) powdered confectioners' sugar
- 1/2 teaspoon (2.5 ml) baking soda
- 1/2 teaspoon (2.5 ml) citric acid

Ingredients#2

- toothpaste with baking soda
- soda pop

Gross Out #1

Combine all the ingredients. Stand near a sink. Place 1/2 teaspoon (2.5 ml) of the powder on your tongue and mix with your saliva. Open your mouth as the foam forms and stick out your tongue. Rinse your mouth with water afterward.

Gross Out #2

If you aren't too grossed out, try this: Get in front of a sink again. Brush your teeth with a large gob of toothpaste that contains baking soda. Don't spit. Take a swig of soda pop and swirl it in your mouth. Open wide and watch the foam gush from your mouth.

Adult Help

Don't Eat

Blind Taste Test

It's easy to tell the difference between a potato and an apple. Or is it? Try this with your family or friends.

WHAT YOU WILL NEED

Ingredients

- firm apple
- onion
- potato
- carrot
- radish

Equipment

- knife
- toothpicks
- blindfold

1. Have an adult cut tiny cubes (about the size of the fingernail on your pinky) of each of the food items in the ingredients list.

2. Poke a toothpick into each cube.

3. Ask a friend to give you a hand with this step. Blindfold your friend and ask him to identify each of the food items you are going to give him to taste. Make sure your friend has no food allergies.

4. Have your friend taste each of the cubes while holding his nose. If your friend does not hold his nose, the activity won't work. Can your friend identify which food is being fed to him? Try the same experiment with a different friend. Did you get the same results?

Adult Help

Honey, I Blew Up the Diaper

Inside every unused diaper there is an exciting science experiment. Disposable diapers contain a harmless chemical, a white powder called sodium polyacrylate. It is science magic just waiting to happen. Add a little water and presto!

What You Will Need

Ingredients

- 1/2 cup (.12 l) water

Equipment

- disposable diaper
- plastic bag

1. Rip open the diaper and place the absorbent part in a plastic bag. Shred the absorbent batting by pulling it apart. You should notice a white powder beginning to collect in the bottom of the bag.

2. When the batting is well shredded, remove the batting and leave the powder in the bag.

3. Add the water to the powder in the bag and watch what happens! The powder absorbs many times its own volume of water. When you are finished, tie the bag and throw it away in the garbage.

Adult Help

Don't Eat

Exploding Soap

Turn an ordinary bar of soap into a strange, growing, flowing creature. Bet you've never seen anything like this!

WHAT YOU WILL NEED

Ingredients

- bar of Ivory Soap®

Equipment

- knife
- large glass microwave-safe container

1. Have an adult cut the bar of soap into four pieces.

2. Place one of the pieces of soap in a glass container.

3. Put the container (uncovered) in the microwave.

4. Have an adult set the microwave for 1 minute. Stand back and watch the fun!

5. Allow the soap to cool for a few minutes before removing it from the microwave.

6. Use this frothy guck when you take a bath or shower.

Adult Help

Don't Eat

•BUBBLES & BLOWERS•

There's nothing like bubbles to cheer up a dreary day. You never need to purchase any from a store, however, since all the ingredients to make great bubbles are probably in your kitchen.

What You Will Need

Ingredients

- water
- glycerine or white corn syrup
- dishwashing liquid

Equipment

- jar with lid
- spoon

Here's the basic formula:

For each cup (.24 l) of water, add 1 tablespoon (14.8 ml) glycerine or white corn syrup and 1/3 cup (.08 l) dishwashing liquid. Combine in a jar and stir to mix.

Things you need to know about bubbles:

- When a wet bubble touches a dry surface, it will burst.
- You can predict when a floating bubble is going to burst by watching the color changes on the surface of the bubble.
- Different amounts of glycerine will affect the strength of your bubble. More glycerine makes stronger bubbles, but using too much will make the liquid too thick and you won't be able to blow bubbles at all.
- Make your own bubble blowers from just about anything around the kitchen. Straws, a leftover plastic fruit basket, a potato masher—even your hand makes a good blower.
- Always keep a damp cloth nearby in case you get any bubbles in your eyes.

Adult Help

Don't Eat